Search and Rescue Dogs

Contents

Written by Chris Oxlade

Dogs saving lives

Search and rescue dogs help to find people who are in danger.

A person called a handler
tells the dog where
to search. The dog
and the handler work
as a team.

The dogs

All dogs have a fantastic sense of smell. Search and rescue dogs learn to use their sense of smell skilfully. They can sniff where a person has been, and lead a rescue team to a **casualty**.

Some types of dog are very clever, and learn these skills quickly. This is why they are chosen to be rescue dogs.

Search and rescue dogs must be brave.

4

Dogs use their sensitive hearing to help find casualties.

Some dogs are strong swimmers.

Training search and rescue dogs

Search and rescue dogs are taught how to climb difficult objects, and how to squeeze into small spaces.

They play hide and seek games.
They practise in the daytime and
at night, whatever the weather.
All these skills help them to find
people who are lost or trapped.

Searching buildings

Search and rescue dogs look and listen for people trapped after earthquakes.

Dogs can squeeze into gaps that are too small for human rescuers.

9

Mountain rescue

Search and rescue dogs also help
to find people who are missing
in the mountains.

Dogs are fast runners. They can search a big area much more quickly than a person can.

Avalanche rescue

Dogs can even smell a person under the snow. They help find **skiers** and mountain climbers trapped by **avalanches**.

Dogs can dig
quickly in
the snow.

Water rescue dogs

Some dogs are trained to rescue people who have fallen into water. Newfoundland dogs are strong swimmers, and they make good water rescue dogs.

These dogs jump into the water from boats, and sometimes from helicopters.

Dog equipment

Search and rescue dogs wear tough boots when they walk over **rubble**. The boots stop their paws from getting cut.

They also wear a **harness** so they can be lifted up or lowered down.

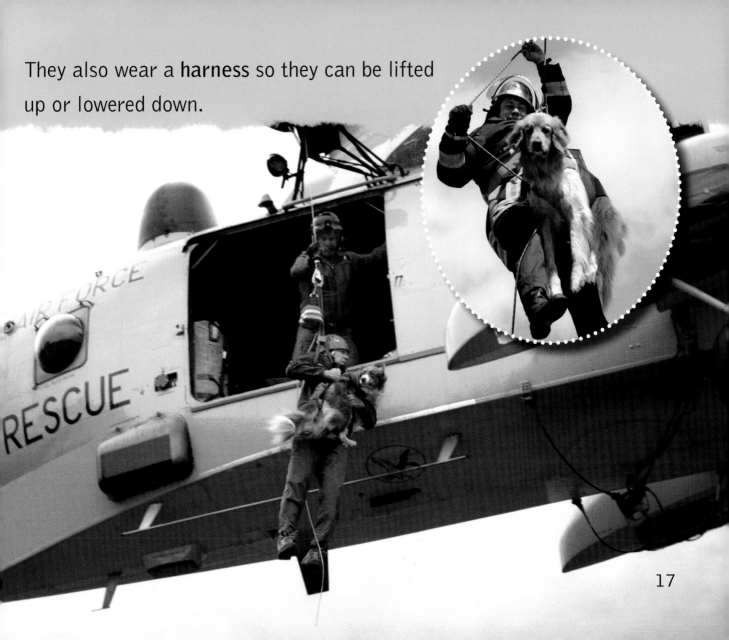

Search and rescue teams

Dogs often work with large search and rescue teams.

Sometimes they travel to other countries to help rescue people. They're used to flying in planes and helicopters.

Gold medals

Sometimes, dogs win medals for their hard work and bravery.

These dogs both won gold medals. Dylan won his medal for saving four people lost in the mountains. Cracker won his medal for searching for people after an earthquake.

Neil Powell and his dogs receiving their awards

Glossary

avalanches   when large amounts of snow slip down the side
                          of a mountain

casualty   someone who has been hurt in an accident

harness   a strap that supports or holds a person or animal

rubble   broken bricks and other old building materials

skiers   people who slide across snow on flat blades called skis

Index

Search and rescue skills

digging skills

brave

good sense
of smell

strong
swimming

good hearing

fast running

Ideas for reading

Written by Gillian Howell
Primary Literacy Consultant

Learning objectives: *(reading objectives correspond with Orange band; all other objectives correspond with Ruby band)* read independently and with increasing fluency longer and less familiar texts; identify and summarise evidence from a text to support a hypothesis; offer reasons and evidence for their views, considering alternative opinions

Curriculum links: Citizenship

Interest words: rescue, mountain, avalanche, equipment, danger, casualty, earthquakes, skiers, helicopters

Resources: pens, paper, whiteboard

Word count: 331

Getting started

- Read the title together and discuss the cover photo with the children. Ask them to say what they think might have happened in the photo and what the dog is doing.

- Turn to the back cover and read the blurb together. Discuss in what situations search and rescue dogs might be needed. Make a note of their suggestions on the whiteboard.

- Turn to the contents page and read the headings with the children. Ask them if they think the book should be read in sequence or dipped into.

Reading and responding

- Ask the children to read the book quietly and make a note of skills that dogs need so they can be effective search and rescue dogs.

- On pp4–5, ensure the children read the captions to the photos. Explain that the captions provide them with further information about the topic and explain why the photos have been used here.

- Remind the children to make use of a variety of strategies to work out any tricky words, e.g. segmenting and blending, looking for words within words and contextual clues.